Sorting objects

Objects can be sorted in different ways,
for example by shape, colour or size.

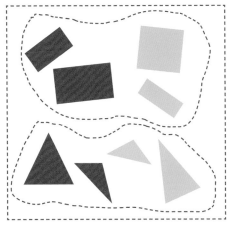

Sorted by shape ↗

Sorted by colour ↗

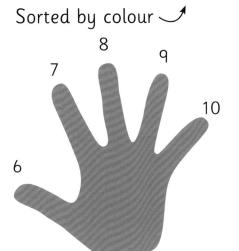

2 3 8 9
   4   7
1   5 6   10

Cardinal n...

one	1	●
two	2	●●
three	3	●●●
four	4	●●●●
five	5	●●●●●
six	6	●●●●● ●
seven	7	●●●●● ●●
eight	8	●●●●● ●●●
nine	9	●●●●● ●●●●
ten	10	●●●●● ●●●●●

Ordinal numbers

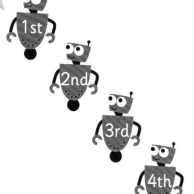

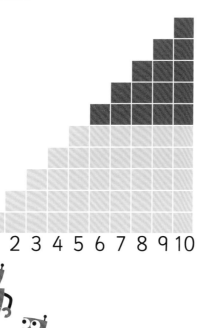

1 2 3 4 5 6 7 8 9 10

1st	first
2nd	second
3rd	third
4th	fourth
5th	fifth
6th	sixth
7th	seventh
8th	eighth
9th	ninth
10th	tenth

Number Symbols

<	=	>
less than	equal to	greater than
6 < 8	8 = 8	10 > 8

Remember – the "small" end always points to the smaller number.

Small **< Big   Big >** Small

Number lines

The number line starts at 0.

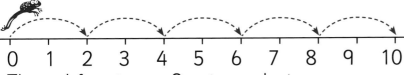

0 1 2 3 4 5 6 7 8 9 10

The green frog jumps 1 unit each time.

It jumps 10 times to reach 10.

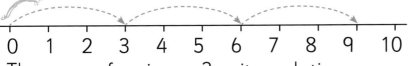

0 1 2 3 4 5 6 7 8 9 10

The red frog jumps 2 units each time.

It jumps 5 times to reach 10.

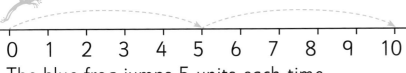

0 1 2 3 4 5 6 7 8 9 10

The orange frog jumps 3 units each time.

It jumps 3 times to reach 9.

0 1 2 3 4 5 6 7 8 9 10

The blue frog jumps 5 units each time.

It jumps twice to reach 10.

Inequalities

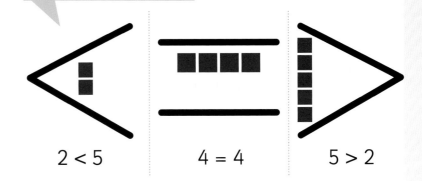

2 < 5   4 = 4   5 > 2

Ten frames

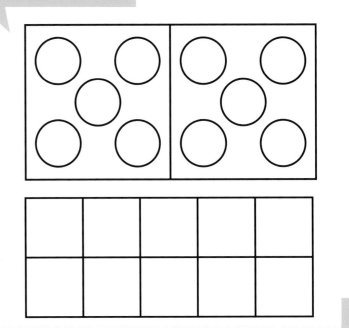

3

Partitioning tree

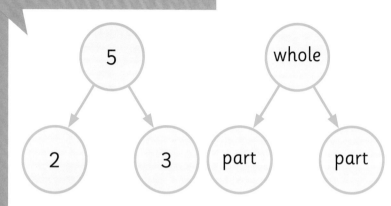

Bar model

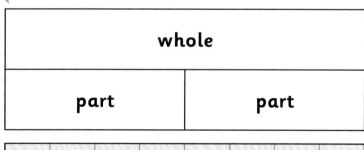

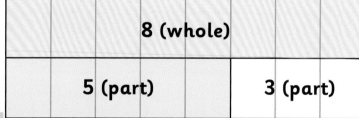

Adding on a number line

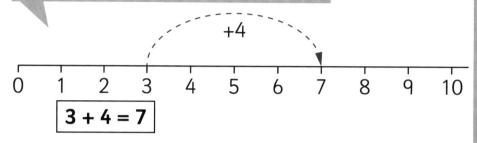

$3 + 4 = 7$

Subtracting on a number line

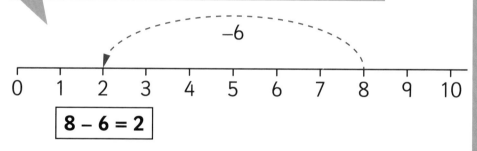

$8 - 6 = 2$

Adding and subtracting on a number line

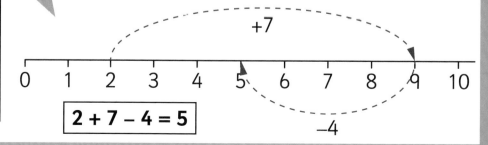

$2 + 7 - 4 = 5$

Pan balance

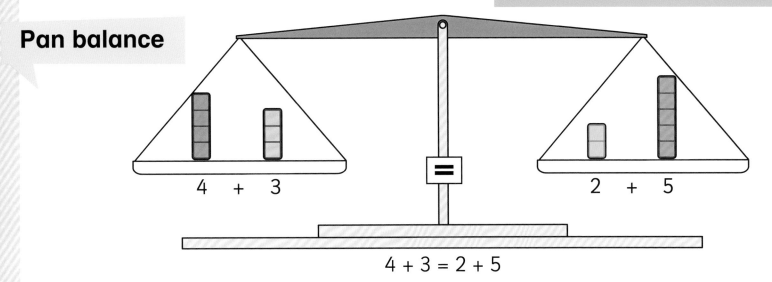

4 + 3

2 + 5

4 + 3 = 2 + 5

Function machine

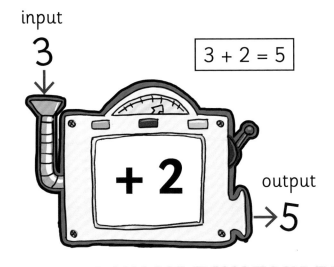

input

3

3 + 2 = 5

+ 2

output

→5

Mapping diagrams

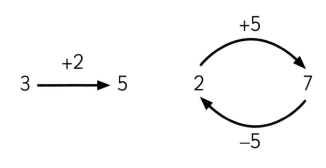

+2

3 ⟶ 5

+5

2   7

−5

Numbers 11–20

11 = 10 + 1
11 is equal to 10 and 1 more

11	
10	1

12 = 10 + 2
12 is equal to 10 and 2 more

12	
10	2

13 = 10 + 3
13 is equal to 10 and 3 more

13	
10	3

14 = 10 + 4
14 is equal to 10 and 4 more

14	
10	4

15 = 10 + 5
15 is equal to 10 and 5 more

15	
10	5

16 = 10 + 6
16 is equal to 10 and 6 more

16	
10	6

17 = 10 + 7
17 is equal to 10 and 7 more

17	
10	7

18 = 10 + 8
18 is equal to 10 and 8 more

18	
10	8

19 = 10 + 9
19 is equal to 10 and 9 more

19	
10	9

20 = 10 + 10
20 is equal to two 10s

20	
10	10

Adding and subtracting on a number line

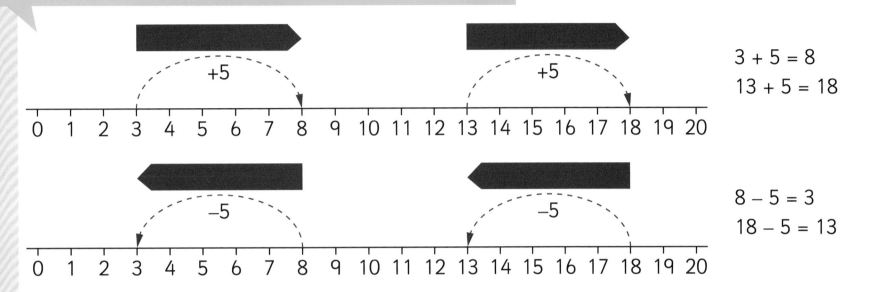

$3 + 5 = 8$

$13 + 5 = 18$

$8 - 5 = 3$

$18 - 5 = 13$

Using number lines and step diagrams to add using the bridging method

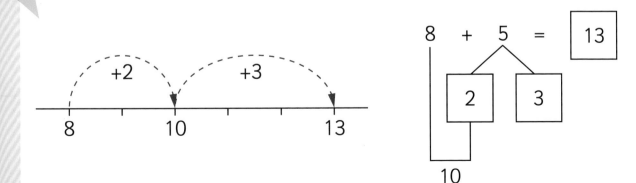

$8 + 5 = 13$

7

Using number lines and step diagrams to subtract using the bridging method

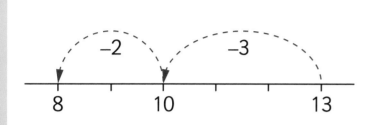

is the same as

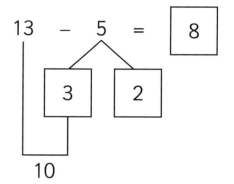

?	
12	3

$12 + 3 = ?$

addend + addend = sum

part + part = whole

15	
?	3

$15 - 3 = ?$

minuend − subtrahend = difference

whole − part = part

Name	Sphere	Cylinder	Cube	Cuboid	Tetrahedron	Square-based pyramid
Number of faces	1 curved surface	2 and 1 curved surface	6	6	4	5
Number of edges	0	0	12	12	6	8
Number of vertices	0	0	8	8	4	5

How many faces?

How many vertices?

How many edges?

Which can roll? Why?

equilateral
triangle

isosceles
triangle

scalene
triangle

right-angled
triangle

decagon

dodecagon

How many triangles
can you see?

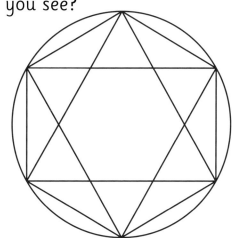

half = $\frac{1}{2}$

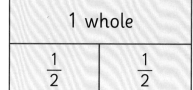

$\frac{1}{2}$ of 6 = 3

quarter = $\frac{1}{4}$

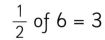

$\frac{1}{4}$ of 12 = 3

100 square

1	2	3	4	5	6	7	8	9	10
11	12	13	14	15	16	17	18	19	20
21	22	23	24	25	26	27	28	29	30
31	32	33	34	35	36	37	38	39	40
41	42	43	44	45	46	47	48	49	50
51	52	53	54	55	56	57	58	59	60
61	62	63	64	65	66	67	68	69	70
71	72	73	74	75	76	77	78	79	80
81	82	83	84	85	86	87	88	89	90
91	92	93	94	95	96	97	98	99	100

ten 10s equal 100

Ways of showing 2-digit numbers

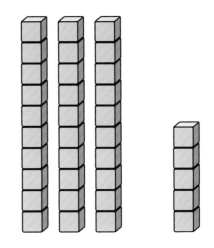

Tens	Ones
● ● ●	● ● ● ● ●

Tens place	Ones place
3	5

$$35 = 30 + 5$$

Numbers on a number line

Where is 56?

Find the tens family.

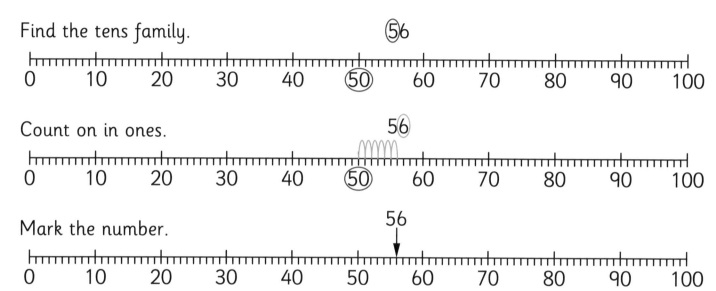

Count on in ones.

Mark the number.

Comparing numbers

2 < 3

3 = 3

3 > 2

Money

| 1p | 2p | 5p | 10p | 20p | 50p | £1 | £2 |

£5

£10

£20

£50

Seasons

Winter   Spring   Summer   Autumn

2018 Calendar

January 2018

S	M	T	W	T	F	S
	1	2	3	4	5	6
7	8	9	10	11	12	13
14	15	16	17	18	19	20
21	22	23	24	25	26	27
28	29	30	31			

February 2018

S	M	T	W	T	F	S
				1	2	3
4	5	6	7	8	9	10
11	12	13	14	15	16	17
18	19	20	21	22	23	24
25	26	27	28			

March 2018

S	M	T	W	T	F	S
				1	2	3
4	5	6	7	8	9	10
11	12	13	14	15	16	17
18	19	20	21	22	23	24
25	26	27	28	29	30	31

April 2018

S	M	T	W	T	F	S
1	2	3	4	5	6	7
8	9	10	11	12	13	14
15	16	17	18	19	20	21
22	23	24	25	26	27	28
29	30					

May 2018

S	M	T	W	T	F	S
		1	2	3	4	5
6	7	8	9	10	11	12
13	14	15	16	17	18	19
20	21	22	23	24	25	26
27	28	29	30	31		

June 2018

S	M	T	W	T	F	S
					1	2
3	4	5	6	7	8	9
10	11	12	13	14	15	16
17	18	19	20	21	22	23
24	25	26	27	28	29	30

July 2018

S	M	T	W	T	F	S
1	2	3	4	5	6	7
8	9	10	11	12	13	14
15	16	17	18	19	20	21
22	23	24	25	26	27	28
29	30	31				

August 2018

S	M	T	W	T	F	S
			1	2	3	4
5	6	7	8	9	10	11
12	13	14	15	16	17	18
19	20	21	22	23	24	25
26	27	28	29	30	31	

September 2018

S	M	T	W	T	F	S
						1
2	3	4	5	6	7	8
9	10	11	12	13	14	15
16	17	18	19	20	21	22
23	24	25	26	27	28	29
30						

October 2018

S	M	T	W	T	F	S
	1	2	3	4	5	6
7	8	9	10	11	12	13
14	15	16	17	18	19	20
21	22	23	24	25	26	27
28	29	30	31			

November 2018

S	M	T	W	T	F	S
				1	2	3
4	5	6	7	8	9	10
11	12	13	14	15	16	17
18	19	20	21	22	23	24
25	26	27	28	29	30	

December 2018

S	M	T	W	T	F	S
						1
2	3	4	5	6	7	8
9	10	11	12	13	14	15
16	17	18	19	20	21	22
23	24	25	26	27	28	29
30	31					

Days of the week

Time

Sunday

Monday

Tuesday

Wednesday

Thursday

Friday

Saturday

 3 o'clock
3:00

 half past 10
10:30

7 o'clock
7:00

half past 7
7:30

half past 8
8:30

1. Getting up

 **2.** Having breakfast

3. Getting to school

12 o'clock
12:00

half past 3
3:30

8 o'clock
8:00

 **4.** Lunchtime

5. Leaving school

6. Bedtime

15

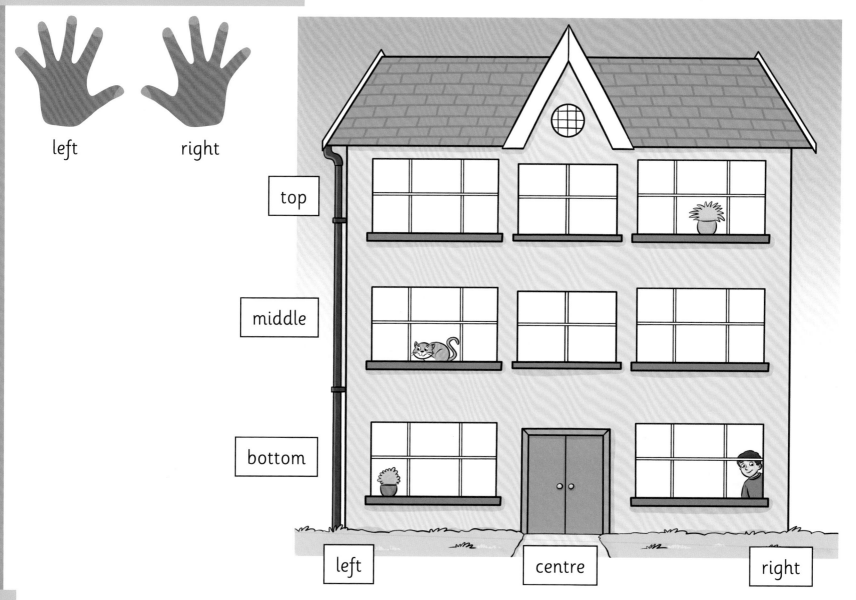

left

right

top

middle

bottom

left

centre

right

The rabbit is next to the hamster.

tallest   shortest

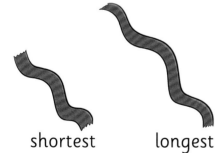

shortest   longest

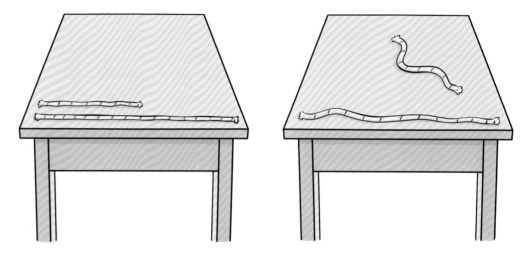

You need to line up the ends of the string to compare them.

You use a ruler to measure short lengths.

You use metre sticks to measure longer lengths and heights.

There are 100 centimetres in 1 metre.

£5 note: a banknote that has a value of £5

£10 note: a banknote that has a value of £10

£20 note: a banknote that has a value of £20

£50 note: a banknote that has a value of £50

above: the bird is above the cat

above

add: increase one number by another or put two numbers together

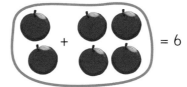

= 6

addend: the number being added, or added to, in an addition calculation, addend + addend = sum

4 + 3 = 7

addend

addition: join or put together two or more numbers or values

after: follows, happens later

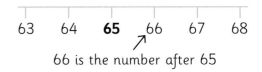

66 is the number after 65

afternoon: the time between morning and evening

altogether: all, everything

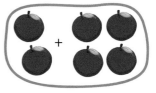

everything

analogue clock: a clock with moving hands and hours marked from 1 to 12 to show you the time

autumn: Autumn is the season between summer and winter. September, October and November are the autumn months.

balanced: equivalent in value

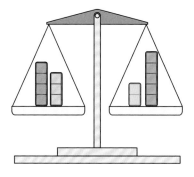

bar model: a diagram to show how wholes are partitioned into parts

9	
4	5

bead string: a string of beads, usually 10, 20, 50 or 100, used to support calculations

before: happens earlier

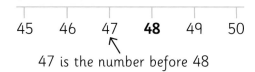

47 is the number before 48

below: the cat is below the bird

below

beside: next to

the red car is beside the yellow car

between: has something on both sides of it

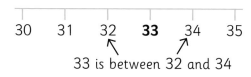

33 is between 32 and 34

bottom: the lowest in a series or pile that is set out vertically

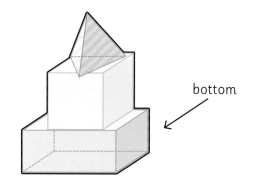

bottom

calculate: work out the answer to a number question

calculation: number statement or number sentence

$$3 + 6 = 9$$
$$7 - 2 = 5$$

cardinal numbers: counting numbers, one, two, three, four, and so on

1, 2, 3, 4, 5, 6, 7, 8, 9, 10

centimetre: small unit of measure; there are 100 centimetres in 1 metre

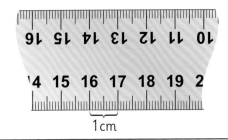

1cm

centre: the middle point

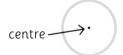

centre

change: the amount you get back when you have paid too much

check: make sure that something is correct

circle: a closed 2-D shape with one side

clock: a device for measuring time

coin: flat piece of metal used as money

combine: join or put together 2 or more quantities or amounts

commutative: Addition is commutative. It does not matter which order the addends are added in, the sum will always be the same.

$$7 + 3 = 10$$
$$3 + 7 = 10$$

compare: look at 2 or more things and see how they are the same or different

count: read or think the number names in order, saying one number name for each object

count back: start counting part way through the counting sequence, continuing by repeatedly counting one less or fewer

count on: start counting part way through the counting sequence, continuing by repeatedly counting one more

criterion: a rule for sorting objects

cube: a 3D shape with 6 identical square faces, 12 edges and 8 vertices

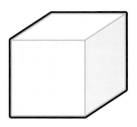

cuboid: a 3-D shape with 6 rectangular faces, 2 of which might be square, 12 edges and 8 vertices

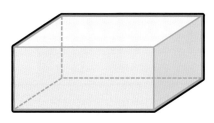

curved surface: not flat, as in the surface of a sphere

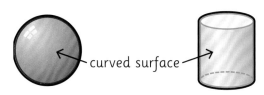
curved surface

cylinder: a 3-D shape with two circular ends and a curved surface joining them

date: the date tells us what day, month and year it is

May 2018						
S	M	T	W	T	F	S
		1	2	3	4	5
6	7	8	9	10	11	12
13	14	15	16	17	18	19
20	21	22	23	24	25	26
27	28	29	30	31		

decagon: any shape with 10 straight sides

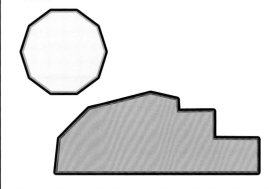

difference: The amount or quantity by which 2 things differ.

The difference between these 2 sticks of cubes is 3 cubes.

digit: any of the symbols 0, 1, 2, 3, 4, 5, 6, 7, 8 or 9

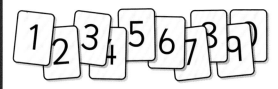

digital clock: a clock with numbers and no hands

dodecagon: any shape with 12 straight sides

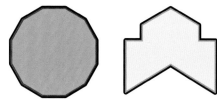

doubling: Adding the same number twice; making something twice as big as it is.

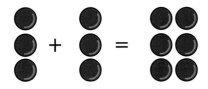

Double 3 is 3 + 3 which is 6.

down: towards a lower position

edge: where two faces meet

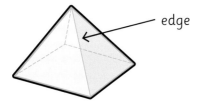

edge

equals: Has the same value. The symbol for equals is =

2 + 2 = 4

equilateral triangle: a triangle with all sides the same length and all vertices the same size

equivalent: has the same value but might have different appearance

$\frac{1}{2} = \frac{2}{4}$ 3 + 4 = 2 + 5

evening: the time at the end of the day, usually from 6pm to midnight

exchange: changing one thing for another

face: the flat surface of a 3-D shape

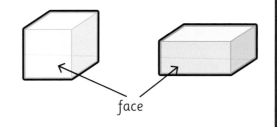

face

first: position number 1

I'm first!

fourth: position number 4

I'm fourth!

function machine: a machine which acts on a number in a particular way, as described by the function

input
3

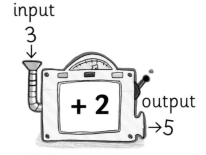

+ 2

output
→5

greater than (>): bigger than, more than

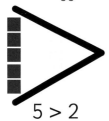

5 > 2

greatest: largest, most, biggest

greatest value: worth the most

5 + 4   8 − 0

greatest value

half past: A time when half an hour has passed since the last o'clock time. The minute hand is on 6 and the hour hand is pointing between two hour numbers.

halving: dividing a quantity into 2 equal parts

Half of 8 is 4

height: how tall something is

height

hour: a period of time that is 60 minutes

hundred square / 100 square: Ten rows of 10 squares. The small squares might be empty or might contain numbers 1–100 in order.

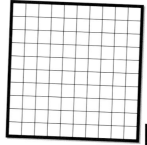

hungarian ten frame: a ten frame with circles arranged in the form of two fives as on a dice, side by side

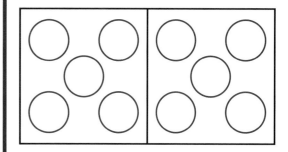

inequality symbol: used to show that 2 numbers or number sentences are not equal in value

< is less than, > is greater than

input: the number going into a function machine

interval: the difference between one number and the next on a number line

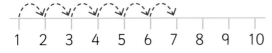

inverse: An operation which reverses another operation. Addition is the inverse of subtraction, doubling is the inverse of halving.

$12 - 4 = 8$

$8 + 4 = 12$

is greater than: shows the larger amount when comparing two quantities

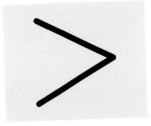

is less than: shows the smaller amount when comparing two quantities

isosceles triangle: a triangle with 2 sides and 2 vertices the same

least: smallest, fewest

least value: worth the least

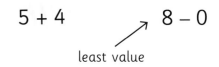

least value

left:

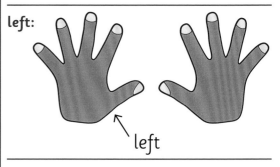

left

length: how long something is; the distance from 1 point to another

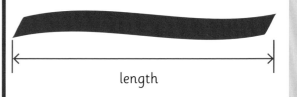

length

less than (<): smaller than, fewer than

$2 < 5$

long: the distance from 1 point to another is not small

long

longer: a greater distance from 1 point to another

long

longer

longest: the greatest distance from 1 point to another

long

longer

longest

match: to be equal to or connected with

measure: to find out how many or how much of something there is

metre: unit of measure equivalent to 100 centimetres

metre stick: Something that is 1 metre long. It might have marks showing each centimetre.

midday: another word for noon; middle of the day; 12 o'clock

middle: a word for between

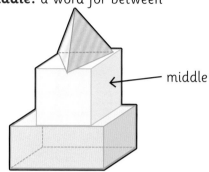

middle

midnight: 12 o'clock during the night, middle of the night. It is also 00:00.

minuend: the whole; the number being subtracted from

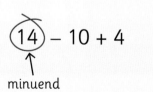

14 – 10 + 4

minuend

minute: A short period of time. There are 60 minutes in an hour.

more than (>): bigger than, greater value than

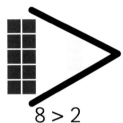

8 > 2

morning: the time between midnight and the afternoon

next to: Another word for beside.

The square is next to the triangle.

---

nil: another word for none, nothing

noon: 12 o'clock during the daytime, separates the morning and afternoon

nought: another name for zero

number bond: a pair of numbers that together make another number

number line: a line of numbers in order, equally spaced and increasing in value from left to right

1 2 3 4 5 6 7 8 9 10

number sentence: sequence of numbers and symbols that describes the value of what is there and how to work it out

8 + 2 =

---

numeral: a symbol that stands for a number

25

o'clock: a time when the minute hand is on 12 and the hour hand is pointing directly to an hour number

one(s): a single thing

ones place: in a 2-digit number, this is the second digit

ones

operation: a mathematical process, often +, −, × or ÷

order: a rule to put things in their correct place

These numbers are in order from least to greatest.

ordinal numbers: numbers that describe position: first, second, third, fourth, and so on

output: the number coming out of a function machine

→ output

pan balance: two pans hung from a central arm can be used to compare quantities of the same objects

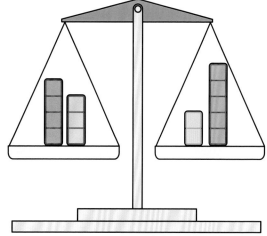

part: a smaller part of a whole number or object

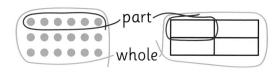

part

whole

partition: split a quantity or number into two or more parts

partitioning tree: a diagram to show how a number has been partitioned

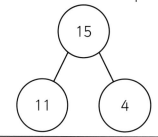

pattern: a regular arrangement of numbers or objects which follow a rule

place value: the value of a digit depends on its place in a number

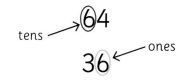

tens

ones

polygon: any shape with three or more straight sides and vertices

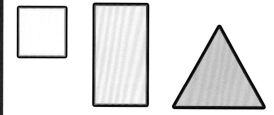

position: Where something is placed.

The pyramid is positioned on the cube.

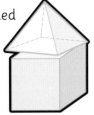

pyramid: a 3-D shape with a polygon-shaped base and triangular sides which meet at a point, or vertex

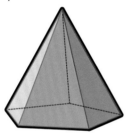

reasoning: thinking carefully about something and explaining it

I know that 3 + 7 makes 10, so 13 + 7 must make 20.

Reasoning

rectangle: any 2-D shape with four sides and four right angles

regular polygon: any 2-D shape with sides of the same length and vertices of the same size

relationship: how one number or object is related to another

right:

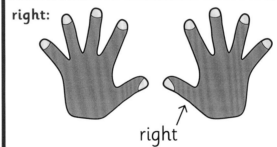

right

right angle: an angle which is equal to a quarter of a turn

roll: to move in a particular direction by turning over and over

row: an arrangement of things all in one line, across the page

rule: the description of how numbers or objects are related

ruler: Something to measure the length of short objects. Usually 15 cm long or 30 cm long. Each centimetre is marked.

scalene triangle: a triangle with all sides and vertices different

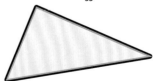

seasons: the year is divided into 4 seasons – winter, spring, summer and autumn

second: position number 2

I'm second!

set: a collection of objects with something in common

short: small distance from one end to the other, not long

short

shorter: smaller distance from one point to another

short

shorter

shortest: smallest distance from one point to another

short

shorter

shortest

slide: to move smoothly across a surface while keeping continuous contact with it

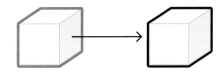

sort: to arrange or group objects according to a rule

sphere: A 3-D shape with a curved surface, no edges or vertices. Every point on the surface is the same distance from the centre.

spring: Spring is the season between winter and summer. March, April and May are the spring months.

square: any 2-D shape with 4 sides of the same length and 4 right angles

square-based pyramid: a pyramid with a square base

subitise: know how many without counting

That's 4 – I don't need to count. I just know there are 4 spots

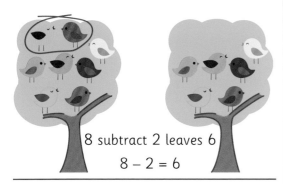

subtract: separate one part from the whole

8 subtract 2 leaves 6

8 – 2 = 6

subtrahend: the number being subtracted from the minuend (or whole)

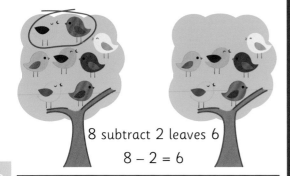

8 subtract 2 leaves 6

8 – 2 = 6

sum: how many altogether after adding

$$4 + 3 = 7$$

sum

summer: Summer is the season between spring and autumn. June, July and August are the summer months.

systematic: working in an orderly manner

table: an arrangement of numbers in rows and columns

input	output
1	3
2	4
3	5
4	6

tall: how high the top of an object is from the ground

tall

taller: the top of the object is higher from the ground than another object

tall   taller

tallest: the top of the object is higher from the ground than all the other objects

tall   taller   tallest

ten frame: a 5 by 2 grid

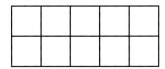

tens number: a number with some tens and no ones (10, 20, 30, and so on)

tens numbers ↓

1	2	3	4	5	6	7	8	9	10
11	12	13	14	15	16	17	18	19	20
21	22	23	24	25	26	27	28	29	30
31	32	33	34	35	36	37	38	39	40
41	42	43	44	45	46	47	48	49	50
51	52	53	54	55	56	57	58	59	60
61	62	63	64	65	66	67	68	69	70
71	72	73	74	75	76	77	78	79	80
81	82	83	84	85	86	87	88	89	90
91	92	93	94	95	96	97	98	99	100

tens place: in a 2-digit number, this is the first digit

tens →

tetrahedron: a pyramid with a triangular base

third: position number 3

I'm third!

today: the day it is now

May 2018

S	M	T	W	T	F	S	
		1	(2)	3	4	5	← today
6	7	8	9	10	11	12	
13	14	15	16	17	18	19	
20	21	22	23	24	25	26	
27	28	29	30	31			

tomorrow: the day after today

May 2018

S	M	T	W	T	F	S	
		1	(2)	(3)	4	5	← today / tomorrow
6	7	8	9	10	11	12	
13	14	15	16	17	18	19	
20	21	22	23	24	25	26	
27	28	29	30	31			

top: the highest point

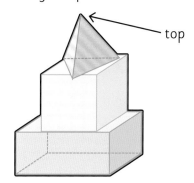

top

total: the whole

triangle: any 2-D shape with 3 sides and vertices

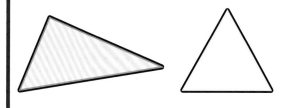

up: towards a higher position

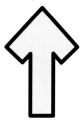

Glossary

value: What something is worth; quantity.

The red counter has a value of 10.
The white counter has a value of 1.

vertex: where 2 sides meet (2-D) or 3 or more edges meet (3-D)

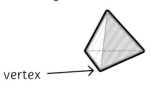

vertex

vertices: More than one vertex

vertices

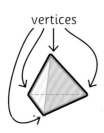

whole: all of something

part

whole

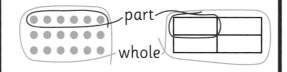

winter: Winter is usually the coldest season. December, January and February are the winter months.

worth: value

the red counter is worth 10 of the white counters

year: a year is 12 months

2018 Calendar

yesterday: the day before today

May 2018						
S	M	T	W	T	F	S
		1	2	3	4	5
6	7	8	9	10	11	12
13	14	15	16	17	18	19
20	21	22	23	24	25	26
27	28	29	30	31		

today
yesterday

zero: no quantity or number, the digit 0